Introduction

Nadia Comaneci is a young girl
from Romania who knows
exactly what she wants and
how to get it.
Gymnastics is the most important
thing in her life.
Ever since she was six years
old, Nadia has trained for at
least four hours a day.
She never complains, and she
practices until she is perfect.
She has no fear of trying
something new.
Today Nadia Comaneci is the
best female gymnast the world
has ever known.

Nadia Comaneci

S. H. Burchard

Illustrated with photographs

Harcourt Brace Jovanovich
New York and London

For Harry Fosha

PHOTO CREDITS

Wide World Photos, cover, pp. 2, 12, 23, 25, 26, 28, 33, 37, 39, 43, 44–45, 47.
Romanian National Tourist Office, pp. 6, 8, 10, 16.
Paris Match, pp. 15, 18, 20, 30, 59, 60, 62–63.
United Press International, 34, 41, 48, 50, 52, 55, 57.

Frontispiece: Romanian gymnast Nadia Comaneci at the Olympic Games in
    Montreal

Printed in the United States of America

First edition

B C D E F G H I J K

Library of Congress Cataloging in Publication Data
Burchard, S   H
    Nadia Comaneci.

    (Sports star)
    SUMMARY: A biography of the Romanian gymnast who received seven per-
fect scores and won four medals at the 1976 Olympics.
    1. Comaneci, Nadia, 1961– —Juvenile literature.   2. Gymnasts—
Romania—Biography—Juvenile literature.   [1. Comaneci, Nadia, 1961–
2. Gymnasts] I. Title.
GV460.2.C65B87   796.4′2′0924 [B] [92]   77–3967
ISBN 0–15–278013–0
ISBN 0–15–684827–9 pbk.

Contents

1

A Child of Romania

Romania is a country in
  southeastern Europe.
If you look for it on a map, you
  will see that it is next to
  Russia.
Hungary, Yugoslavia, and
  Bulgaria are the other
  countries that surround it.
Romania is famous for its
  beautiful snowcapped

One of the many beautiful mountain valleys
in Romania

mountains and the wide rivers
that cut through its mountain
ranges.
Huge castles can be seen on top
of steep mountain cliffs.
The famous Count Dracula lived
in one of these castles.

Romania has a Communist government that runs all the businesses, the farms, the schools, and even the sports events in the country.

Before their children were born, Gheorghe Comaneci and his wife, Alexandrina, lived in a small farm town called Onesti in the foothills of the Carpathian Mountains.

In 1952 the new Soviet Premier Gheorghe Gheorghiu-Dej decided to build a big city at Onesti.

He called it by his own name.

9

The castle of Count Dracula

All the old peasant houses were
  torn down.
Big blocks of apartment houses
  took their place.

The modern city of Gheorghe Gheorghiu-Dej
was once a farm village.

New schools, factories, stores,
  and fine athletic buildings
  were also put up.
The Comanecis moved into one of
  the new apartment buildings in
  Gheorghe Gheorghiu-Dej.
Gheorghe Comaneci worked as an
  automobile mechanic repairing
  trucks that were used in the
  nearby forests.
Alexandrina Comaneci worked in
  a hospital.
It was in this brand-new
  Romanian city on
  November 12, 1961, that
  Nadia Comaneci (Nad-ya
  Koh-ma-neech) was born.

Nadia in school

2

Nadia Is Discovered

From a very early age Nadia
  was a fine athlete.
Sometimes her playmates
  would complain.
"It's not fair," they said.
"Nadia always beats us."
She was always running and
  playing—and jumping.
In three years the Comaneci
  family had to buy four couches.

Nadia had jumped on them until
their springs broke.
Her parents were glad when she
went to school and could jump
in the school gym.
When Nadia was old enough to go
to kindergarten, gymnastics
was part of the school
athletic program.
In fact, the Romanian government
had a strong interest in
gymnastics.
Since its leaders were making
sports an important part of
every child's education, they
made sure that their schools
had good gymnastic programs.

They wanted to show off their athletes at future Olympic Games.

Nadia gives a lesson
to some very small Romanian gymnasts.

The modern sports buildings in which
young Romanian girls learn to become
some of the world's finest gymnasts

A big, modern sports high
school, where the best women
gymnasts in the country could
go to school and train, was
built in Gheorghe Gheorghiu-
Dej—Nadia's hometown.
Bela and Marta Karoly—
a husband and wife—were
coaches at the new school.
They believed that to be a great
gymnast you had to begin
training at five or six years
of age.
So they set off on a search for
young athletes.
One day Bela Karoly came to
Nadia's school.

He saw Nadia and a friend
   playing at gymnastics at
   recess.
He could see that Nadia had
   great skill, but then the bell
   rang.

In the rush of changing classes,
   he lost sight of her.
Mr. Karoly ran from room to
   room looking for Nadia.
He could not find her.
Finally, on his third trip to
   all the classrooms, he poked
   his head in a door and shouted,
   "Who loves gymnastics here?"
"We, we!" cried Nadia and a
   friend, leaping up from their
   desks.

Marta and Bela Karoly
with their star pupil

3

Training to Be the Best

From that day on, Marta and Bela
   Karoly were like second
   parents to Nadia.
They coached her for at least
   four hours every day.
She was one of a group of twenty-
   six little girls that the Karolys
   picked out.
They chose carefully.

In her school uniform, Nadia poses
in front of the sports high school.

They hoped to be able to put
together a team of the finest
women gymnasts in the world.
The training began at once.
When Nadia was seven, the
Karolys entered her in the
National Championship of
Romania.
Nadia was the youngest girl in
the tournament.
She placed thirteenth.
Her coaches were pleased.
But would being number
thirteen be unlucky for her?
Bela Karoly bought Nadia an
Eskimo doll to bring her good
luck.

Coach Bela Karoly watches best friends
Teodora Ungureanu and Nadia join hands.

The next year Nadia came in
number one and never lost
again.

The doll had nothing to do with
the victory, of course, but
Nadia carried it to every
tournament she entered.
Everywhere she went, she began
to collect dolls.
When she was not in training or
competing, Nadia was like any
other child.
She played tricks on her friends
at recess.
At home she played with her
dolls and rode her bicycle.
She liked to tease her younger
brother, Adrian.
One day Nadia and her best
friend, Teodora Ungureanu

24

(also a gymnast), held hands
and threw Adrian all the way
up to the ceiling, where he
left two dirty fingerprints.
"I was not afraid," said Nadia's
little brother.

Alexandrina Comaneci with her children
Adrian and Nadia

The girls often played soccer
   with the boys.
The losers had to buy chocolate
   bars for the winners.
Nadia and Teodora won many
   chocolate bars.
But during her many hours of
   training, Nadia stopped
   behaving like a child.
She became very serious.
She knew she was doing
   something important.
She had a lot of courage.
No exercise was ever too
   difficult for her to learn.
Every time she started to learn
   a new routine, her coaches

Nadia sometimes plays ball with the boys.

would hold her and guide her body.

Soon Nadia could do the routine without help.

Then she would spend hours, and even days, doing the moves over and over until everything was perfect.

Nadia shows her perfect form on the balance beam in this triple exposure.

It was not long before it became clear that Nadia Comaneci could be one of the greatest gymnasts the world has ever seen.

The team that trained her grew to include not only the Karolys, her coaches, but also a choreographer to teach her dance moves, a piano player to accompany her, and a doctor and a masseur to take care of her well-trained body.

A serious little champion

4

The 1976 Olympic Games

By the time she was eleven years
   old, Nadia began winning one
   championship after another.
First she won the 1973
   Championship of Romania.
That same year she won the
   Tournament of Friendship in
   Moscow.
In London early in 1975 she won
   the Champions Tournament.

Later that year came Nadia's greatest moment.

In a small town in Norway, Nadia won the tournament that made her the champion of Europe.

At fourteen she was the youngest champion in the eighteen-year history of the event.

She weighed only 86 pounds and was not even five feet tall.

The following summer Nadia and the Romanian Olympic team went to Montreal, Canada, to compete in the 1976 Olympic Games.

Nadia's parents took her to the airport.

Nadia as she gets ready
to board the airplane

They did not have enough money
to go with her.
Nadia did not seem to be her
usual self at the airport.

Her parents could see
     that their usually calm
     daughter would not talk to
     anyone.
A few days later they got a
     postcard from Montreal.

In her good handwriting Nadia
told her parents that she was
fine.
She wrote about the big hotel
where the team was living
and about the city of
Montreal.
She mentioned her long hours
of practice.
Best of all, Nadia told her
parents she was sure that
she would do well.
Nadia's parents felt better.
"If Nadia says it will be O.K.,"
said her father, "then it will
be O.K."

The Romanian girls choose postcards
to send home.

Nadia was calm and sure of
  herself.
She knew her routines perfectly.
After all, she had been working
  on them for eight years.
On the floor of the arena were
  the four familiar areas in
  which she must perform.
At one end was the balance beam
  —a long wooden bar raised
  4½ feet off the ground.
The uneven parallel bars stood
  at the other end of the arena.
In between, side by side, were
  the horse vault and the large
  orange mat used for floor
  exercises.

Nadia holds a new doll and talks
to a television reporter in Montreal
as her coach Bela Karoly looks on.

There were only women on the
  floor.
No male coaches were allowed.
The judges were all women.
So were all the assistants and
  messengers.
The only men allowed were the
  piano players.
Routines were performed in all
  four areas at once.
It was like watching a four-ring
  circus.
But soon all eyes were on Nadia.
On the uneven bars she whirled
  from bar to bar as easily as
  a bird flutters from limb to
  limb on a tree.

The crowd held its breath.
Never had they seen such daring
    performed with such perfection.

Nadia performing
on the uneven parallel bars

The four women judges gave their
votes to a little girl runner.
The runner carried the votes to
a woman with a long pole.
The score was written on a sign,
mounted on the pole, and
shown to the audience.
A perfect score of 10.0!
The crowd exploded with cheers.
Nadia was the first Olympic
gymnast ever to be given a
perfect score.
Nadia did not seem surprised.
"I know it was perfect," she
said.
After all, she had done it
many times before.

Nadia lifts her arms in victory
after being given a perfect score.

Nadia went on to score three
more perfect tens on the
uneven bars during the rest
of the week.

She was just as good on the
balance beam.

The balance beam is the piece of
equipment that frightens
gymnasts the most.

It is very easy to fall off
while doing difficult
exercises.

Nadia's complete control on the
beam kept the audience in
hushed silence.

In a minute and a half she
jumped on the four-inch-wide

beam, did a handstand, twirled
and skipped, did several fancy
dance steps, a back walkover,
cartwheels, split leaps into
the air, and a double
somersault to get off.

An amazing Nadia
on the balance beam

A multiple exposure shows Nadia doing
the balance beam routine that
won her a gold medal.

Not once did she wobble.
Another perfect score of 10.0!
Everyone in the arena stood and
    cheered for several minutes.
They had never seen anyone give
    such a perfect performance.
Nadia scored two more perfect
    tens on the beam.
For her performance on the horse
    vault, Nadia had to race down
    the floor, jump on a spring-
    board, and fly to the horse.
She landed hands first and
    pushed off quickly to her feet.
Long ago Greek athletes vaulted
    over the horns of live bulls
    for this event.

Nadia's highest score was a 9.85
— not quite perfect.

Nadia has a determined look on her face
as she flies toward the horse.

The floor exercises are a
combination of tumbling and
dancing.

Nadia's piano player played a
   lively "Yes, Sir, That's My
   Baby" as she moved gracefully
   through her routine.
She looked like part ballerina
   and part cheerleader.
Her best score for this exercise
   was a nearly perfect 9.9.
On the third night of the
   competition, fourteen-year-old
   Nadia Comaneci was awarded a
   gold medal for being the best
   all-around gymnast in the
   world.
As the large medal was placed
   around her neck, Nadia smiled
   and raised her arms.

A graceful Nadia struts to the tune of
"Yes, Sir, That's My Baby."

The winner!

She was the best and she knew it.
She had given the most amazing
    gymnastic performance ever
    seen.
And there was more to come.

5

Back to School

Nadia came back to Romania with
   three gold medals, a bronze,
   and seven perfect scores.
She had been the star of the
   1976 Olympic Games.
Her friend Teodora Ungureanu
   also had very high scores.
The rest of the Olympic
   gymnastic team had done well,
   too.

Nadia waves to the huge crowd who came
to meet her at the Bucharest airport
when she returned to Romania.

Thousands of Romanians rushed
onto the airfield at Bucharest
when the team returned.
They stormed the gangway as the
plane landed.
The door of the plane stayed
closed for fifteen minutes
while the police cleared a
path for Nadia and her seven
teammates.
A few days later a ceremony took
place in the new Palace of
Sports and Culture in
Romania's capital city,
Bucharest.
Nadia and Teodora and the rest
of the team were there.

A champion poses with her parents,
Alexandrina and Gheorghe Comaneci.

The President of Romania,
Nicolae Ceausescu, praised the
Olympic team and then leaned
over and placed yet another
medal around Nadia's neck.
She was awarded the long title
of Hero of Socialist Labor and
the gold Hammer and Sickle
Medal.
It was the highest honor that is
given in Romania.
The President and his wife each
gave Nadia a kiss.
The whole world kept heaping
praise on Nadia.
An hour-long television special,
hosted by Flip Wilson, was

filmed in Romania and shown
in the United States in
November of 1976.

Teodora and Nadia
give TV star
Flip Wilson
a few pointers.

People from all over the world
sent her letters and dolls.
Some people change when they
become famous.
But for the Comaneci family,
life is the same as before
Nadia became the most famous
fourteen-year-old in the world.
She is a full-time student at
the Gheorghe Gheorghiu-Dej
Sports High School.
Each morning at eight Nadia
begins her first class.
She has twenty-five classmates
who are all girls.
They all wear navy blue dresses
with light blue blouses.

Nadia recites in class.

"Nadia is good in English, in natural science, and she sings very well in French," says her principal.

Nadia puts on a fancy Romanian blouse over her school uniform.

Nadia goes to classes until noon,
  and at two o'clock she heads
  for the gym.
She puts on her shoes, which are
  like ballet slippers.
She puts on her tights.
With a serious look on her face,
  Nadia listens to her coaches.
Even though she is a world
  champion, she obeys everything
  they say and never complains.
When Marta Karoly says, "Let's
  go to work now!" Nadia takes
  a deep breath and begins her
  routine.
All of a sudden she starts
  flying dancing on the bars.

All the muscles in her body seem
to be moving at once.
As they watch her, sometimes her
coaches are silent.

Nadia thinks carefully about
what she is doing
as Coach Karoly watches.

Other times they give her orders
in a low voice, "Move your
head . . . you tremble too
much when you land."

Sometimes they look upon the
child they have trained with
awe.

It is difficult to imagine how
good she will be in the next
Olympic Games.

When people ask Nadia what she
wants to do most, she gets
very serious and says, "I want
to keep improving."

When Nadia says something, she
means it.